ANNUAL SHAKESPEARE LECTURE

THE MYTHICAL SORROWS OF SHAKESPEARE

By C. J. SISSON

Read 25 April 1934

ANNUAL SHAKESPEARE LECTURE

THE MYTHICAL SORROWS OF SHAKESPEARE

By C. J. SISSON

Read 25 April 1934

IT may seem to some lovers of Shakespeare that other lovers of Shakespeare have of late been usurping divine functions. In the beginning, God created man in his own image, we are told in Holy Writ. And Shakespeare is to me an important piece of evidence that there is some truth in this statement. But much that has been written about Shakespeare suggests a desire to re-create Shakespeare into an image more satisfactory to the critic writing, sometimes inclining towards self-portraiture. This is no new complaint. Long ago the German critic Gervinus inveighed against his fellow-countrymen, the creators of a Shakespeare after *their* image:

Diese Kritiker trugen ihre eigene Verworrenheit und Blasirtheit in die kräftige Natur hinüber, deren Maas in der That ihnen nicht gegeben war.

These are bitter words. But the time seems to have come to recall them, and to invite agreement to the proposition that some of the writings of more recent critics labour under the same kind of error as those of the predecessors and contemporaries of Gervinus, upon whom this judgement fell.

The present generation of German students of Shakespeare affords a striking example of what has been recently pleaded for, in eloquent language, by a poet-scholar, Professor Lascelles Abercrombie, when he lectured before the British Academy upon the Liberty of Interpretation. The latest volume of the *Shakespeare Jahrbuch* is permeated throughout by determined and ardent propaganda, by dint of which there arises, as from a trap-door at Bayreuth, a

1

dour heroic figure of pure Nordic ancestry, the enemy of all Southern decadences, faithful to his Leader, the prophet of the new Germany of to-day. For him, for example, 'ripeness is all'. It is represented that man's life comes to its true fulfilment, as Shakespeare sees it, when he arrives at the supreme moment of self-immolation on the altar of his national and private ideals of patriotism, loyalty, and honour. It is not a little disconcerting, if not indeed alarming. But is it any more disconcerting than the Shakespeare who emerges from the sorry mists of a depressed post-war outlook upon life on this side of the protecting Channel; the outcome of twentieth-century blues, which lay hold of Shakespeare as a fellow-sufferer from pessimism and disillusionment, a victim of seventeenth-century blues? On the whole, if we must choose between two such Shakespeares, we might well prefer the Teutonic hero to the Anglo-Slavic waif of time and fate, imported from the grievous pages of Russian fiction. There is something to be said, after all, for Carlyle's notion that a nation may be judged by what it makes of its great men. But, for the moment, these two warring conceptions of Shakespeare may serve to illustrate the extreme possibilities of liberty of interpretation, as conceived by some men who may justly claim to be in the vanguard of Shakespearian scholarship.

It is perhaps not unreasonable to suggest that the dramatizing of Shakespeare the man has gone too far, when we remember also the picture drawn for us by a score of writers of yet a third Shakespeare, a man shaken by personal passion, moving from mood to mood, from optimism to pessimism and back again to resigned imperturbability. This is not, as might reasonably be imagined, a character to be found only in the pages of the considerable mass of recent drama which has taken advantage of the popular fame of a great figure in literature, and in which creative art is allowed to transcend the tiresome limitations of history or even probability. It is a picture familiar in works of a stricter purpose. So we are bidden once more, by one of the most honoured and exact among Shakespearian scholars of the present day, to observe the gradual revelation of Shakespeare's tragic spiritual life as reflected in his plays from *Hamlet* onwards, reaching its catastrophic disastrous climax when he wrote *Timon of Athens*, the proof of some kind of a break-down, and proceeding by way of some kind of conversion and subsequent convalescence to a renewed strength and faith in which he died.

It is no easy matter to disentangle the threads of the complex mass of argument adduced in favour of these or other modes of exhibiting the man Shakespeare in picturesque terms. A few crumbs of biographical fact or legend find their place, of course, such as the death of Shakespeare's son Hamnet, or Archdeacon Richard Davies's remark that Shakespeare 'died a Papist'. But these are of small weight beside the main lines of argument variously pursued, which rest on four dogmas. First, that the actual evolution of Shakespeare's personal life must be read into his poetic and dramatic work. Second, that dramatists write tragedies when their mood is tragic, and comedies when they are feeling pleased with life. Thirdly, that Shakespeare was so far a child of his own age that he faithfully reflected its spirit in his literary work, and fourthly, that the spirit of the age was heroic and optimistic under Elizabeth, degenerating towards the end of her reign into the cynicism, disillusionment, and pessimism which marked the reign of James the First.

It is not easy to refute dialectic which, when driven back to the end of one limb of its argument, say the biographical interpretation of literary work, can leap lightly on to the limb below, and cling defiantly to the spirit of the age, or clutch one bough with both hands while its feet are lodged on another. And there is always, in the last resort, the reckless climb to precarious heights of intuitive certainty, from which there is no appeal.

It is my belief that the overwhelming deadweight of nineteenth-century criticism of Shakespeare is in the main responsible for the general trend of such interpretative biography to-day. Certainly, our modern writers are perpetuating ideas which are, for the most part, a hundred years old or more. There is much food for thought in the history of the origin and development of the romantic myth which is so familiar to us to-day and bids fair to become established among us with apostolic authority, and which nevertheless may seem to some to be pure delusion.

The eighteenth century was not concerned with Shakespeare the man, except in the way of anecdotage, nor with the personal interpretation of his works. But, towards the end of the century, that great scholar Malone laid the foundations for all subsequent consideration of the possible biographical significances of the plays, when he essayed to establish their chronological order. Nor was it long before Coleridge took the next step, dividing the plays according to periods of their author's life. From 1810 onwards he suggested a variety of systems, mostly arranging the plays under five Epochs, but on one occasion under periods entitled 'Youthful', 'Manly', and 'Mature', setting aside the history plays. There are hints of what was to follow in later writers, for Coleridge, as he states his position himself, is concerned rather with 'physiological and pathological than chronological' order. It is Coleridge who first considers how far Shakespeare's changing moods are reflected in his art, who first, for example, sees *Troilus and Cressida* as the sign of a transition to an ironical frame of mind in its creator. The way is now open to the inevitable elaboration of such hints, and to the systematization of such an approach to Shakespeare's work. It is true that Coleridge insists on Shakespeare's Protean divinity and on his Olympian detachment:

Proteus, a river, a lion, yet still the god felt to be there.

Then his thinking faculty and thereby perfect abstraction from himself; he works exactly as if of another planet, as describing the movements of two butterflies.

But the mischief was done. Moreover, the German Romantics had already entered the field, to some purpose. Friedrich Schlegel was the originator of the Shakespeare who appeals to Nazi Germany as 'rather an old-Northern poet than a Christian poet', one who sees the riddle of life as essentially a 'tragic riddle', in harmony with the present-day doctrine of 'Pantragismus'. Shakespeare's outlook upon life, thus envisaged, was held to be profoundly sceptical, and his bitter realization of the tragic problems of life to have found expression in *King Lear* in 'pain and suffering which swells to madness'. So it is in Shakespeare's own inmost feelings, we are told, that we must seek the key to his tragic spirit And it is Friedrich Schlegel who shows us a Shakespeare utterly out of tune with the world he lived in, save in his patriotism, who wrote plays the true meaning of which was not guessed at even by their actors, much less by any of the spectators. It was fortunate that it was so indeed, we might well interject, for *Hamlet*, as understood by Schlegel, had a suicidal effect, and in 1792 Schlegel himself hovered on the verge for several days after grasping what Shakespeare really meant. Thus was Shakespeare adopted, full blood-brother to all Romantics, and clasped to Friedrich's passionate heart, nearly a hundred and fifty years ago.

Friedrich's brother August, a little later, opened up another fruitful line of imaginative biography. Marvelling how it fell that no editor of Shakespeare had seen the significance of the *Sonnets*, he asserts that they

describe quite obviously real situations and moods of the poet, make us acquainted with the passions of the man himself, indeed contain remarkable confessions of his youthful errors,

for example, with respect to the shame of his life as a player.

Finally, among the founders of this century-old school of biographers, comes the judicious Hallam, who first definitely set the model of the kind of biography that August Schlegel thought so desirable. Thus he wrote in 1837:

There seems to have been a period of Shakespeare's life when his heart was ill at ease, and ill content with the world or his own conscience; the memory of hours misspent, the pang of affection misplaced or unrequited, the experience of man's worser nature which intercourse with unworthy associates, by choice or circumstance, peculiarly teaches;—these, as they sank down into the depths of his great mind, seem not only to have inspired into it the conception of Lear and Timon, but that of one primary character, the censurer of mankind.

As Hallam sees it, this obsession may be traced developing from Jaques in *As You Like It* to the Duke in *Measure for Measure*, on to Hamlet, Lear, and Timon, during the years 1600 to 1604, after which, from *Macbeth* onwards, Shakespeare's later plays are free of it. We may well say that Hallam fairly set the ball rolling. Shakespeare was now well afloat on his posthumous sea of troubles.

Protests were raised, ninety years ago, against such conclusions, both in England and in Germany. Charles Knight, in 1843, quotes Hallam with disapproval, asserting that it is precisely in his great tragedies that we see Shakespeare's genius in its fullest command of itself, and his power in fullest exercise, 'at its very point and culmination'. And Delius in 1847 lays his finger on the more general fallacy of demanding a tragic life to explain tragic creation: no one would believe, he complains, that Shakespeare lived the life of an ordinary mortal:

> The Hero of Romance must not, should not, only have written romantic poetry, but must also have lived a romantic life; not only have created tragedies on the stage, but also have experienced tragedies in his own house; must have loved unhappily like Romeo, and like Hamlet not have known for a time what to get on with next.

But such protests were of little avail against so strongly flowing a tide, the triumph of which was ensured by the immense influence of Dowden's impressive book, *Shakespeare: a Critical Study of his Mind and Art* (1875), which set forth in a more elaborate fashion Coleridge's division of his plays into periods, relating them clearly to the poet's outlook upon his work and upon life. Dowden is careful to guard himself against romanticism, against the notion, for example, that the period of the tragedies was 'a period of depression and gloom in Shakespeare's spiritual progress', or that Shakespeare ever gave way to 'despair of human virtue'. But he paved the way for critics of less wisdom and caution, for whom his book yielded many texts. And indeed, Dowden himself in later years, when writing introductions for the *Oxford Shakespeare*, has eaten of the bitter root himself, and presents the now familiar Shakespeare of *Troilus and Cressida* and *Timon of Athens* who is himself the victim of disillusionment, embittered by the Lady of the Sonnets, seeking relief from his sufferings in dramatic expression, finally overcoming personal indignation, and attaining that serenity of which the last plays are the evidence.

Towards the end of the century strange plants of rhetoric began to shoot upon the seed-plot thus prepared. In 1880 Swinburne bade us observe in *Timon of Athens*

a poem inspired at once by the triune Furies of Ezekiel, of Juvenal, and of Dante,

and presumably by a fourth, the Fury of William Shakespeare himself. And presently even Swinburne's turgid excitement was out-Heroded by Teutonic rivals. Ten Brink in 1893 takes us

into a bleak mountain region with its topmost summits shrouded in mist,

beginning in 1601, when bitterness of spirit supervened, culminating in 'Titanic outbursts of fury' in *Timon*, and giving place to renewed hope after 1607. It appears that in 1607 Shakespeare's brother Edmund died, an event which helped to infuriate him. Fortunately, in 1608 his mother died, an event which restored him to a kindlier mood. So various are the effects of deaths in the family upon a great poet. The birth of a granddaughter helped, of course.

With Brandes in 1896 we reach the full harvest which, it might seem, could leave scope only for gleaners to come. We see the young Shakespeare, his 'life bathed in sunshine', when (at the age of thirty-five, let us observe) 'his whole nature burst into flower'. 'He was doubtless in love at this time,...a happy love.' (Anne Hathaway, poor hobby-horse, a little forgotten.) But there was a latent melancholy in this middle-aged youth, which developed after a short serene period of two or three years, from *Twelfth Night* to *As You Like It*. Eight years of 'lofty contempt for humanity' follow.

By the time Shakespeare had written *Antony and Cleopatra*, his melancholy had deepened into pessimism. ... *Troilus and Cressida* strikes at the relations of the sexes, *Coriolanus* at political life; until all that, in these years, Shakespeare has endured and experienced, thought and suffered, is concentrated into the one great despairing figure of Timon of Athens, 'misanthropos', whose savage rhetoric is like a dark secretion of clotted blood and gall, drawn off to assuage pain.

In *Measure for Measure* Shakespeare, it appears, 'for the first time anticipates Schopenhauer', a feat which to Brandes appeared to be wholly praiseworthy. *King Lear* was the outcome of a chance meeting of an indignant Shakespeare with Holinshed. Abhorrence of human nature, easily traceable in *Antony and Cleopatra*, expands into full bloom in *Troilus and Cressida*. But we are consoled by the later history of the case:

Shakespeare has shouted himself hoarse and his fury is spent. The fever is over and convalescence has set in. The darkened sun shines out once more, and the gloomy sky shines blue again.

Brandes is unable to explain what it was that cured his patient, and laments our ignorance of the relevant facts of Shakespeare's life. He might have remembered Dowden's witty admonition:

It is hardly perhaps a sound method of criticism to invent a hypothesis which creates an insoluble difficulty.

Somehow, at any rate, 'one of the decisive crises of his life' had taken place, and convalescence was the outcome, a condition which, Brandes assures us, is deeply appreciative of life, and serene in outlook. The study of Brandes, indeed, leads one to believe that he has been more widely read than at first sight would seem probable or reasonable. This impression is deepened when we consider his diagnosis of the disease in question. Here he is not troubled by any realization of ignorance.

Shakespeare's latent melancholy, according to Brandes, was developed by a variety of causes. First, he was obliged to associate with Doll Tearsheets and Quicklys, and with bold and illiterate bourgeois women, and never had the advantage of meeting cultured and virtuous ladies. This made him rather bitter. The growth of Puritanism, hostile to the stage and to art, made him more bitter. But what stung him to frenzy was the fall of the Earl of Essex and of Southampton. And here Brandes develops a hint from Ten Brink. Essex, it seems, who was idolized by public opinion, 'had Shakespeare's full personal loyalty' also. The poet resented the Queen's treatment of his heroes so deeply that he fell from cheerfulness into gloom, and revenged himself on Elizabeth by refusing to celebrate her death in verse. Of course, there was also the Dark Lady. She had to be punished too, and she had her deserts on the stage as Cressida and Cleopatra. Here let us leave Brandes. The Essex story is older than Brandes or Ten Brink, of course. Capell had a word about it as long ago as in his Preface of 1768, and Gervinus refers to it in 1849, only to reject it. It is, indeed, as if Mr. Shaw should have taken to writing bitter tragedy when the Socialist government fell in 1931, and his friends Lords Ponsonby and Snowden with it.

There is no need to quote further, from Bradley, or from Furnivall, or from more recent scholars, much less from such romances as those of Mr. Frank Harris or Mr. Frank Mathew, which do little more than to furbish up once again ancient contributions to the imposing saga of the sorrows of Shakespeare. The myth of his melancholy dates from Friedrich Schlegel, and is a hundred and forty years old. The myth of his change from cheerful youth to uneasy middle age dates from Hallam, and is a hundred years old.

The myth which attributes his pessimism to the fall of Essex is the oldest of all, and has a career of over a hundred and sixty years. The history of the saga is, in fact, one of damnable iteration under the guise of novelty. Is it not indeed time to consider the bases upon which this vast mass of authority has been built up?

First, let me deal with the only considerable addition which more recent study has contributed to this edifice, namely the myth which I might compendiously describe as the myth of seventeenth-century blues, in which Shakespeare is submerged. It is a development of the myth of melancholy, extended from the conception of a personal affliction of Shakespeare to that of a universal epidemic in England, and compared with the England of the present post-war age, also seen in a blue light. With this proposition I can only deal very briefly, in the hope of the fuller treatment by more competent authority which it deserves. I will content myself with two observations.

The melancholy which is taken so seriously in this new myth was a general object of mirth and satire to the Elizabethans themselves. It was, in the main, a fashion and an affectation. Lyly poked fun at it in *Midas*, long before any possible post-Armada disillusionment, and long before the depressing James loomed up from Scotland. Ben Jonson was not the only dramatist to make it ridiculous as a formal affectation. Shakespeare's own treatment of the question is invariably mocking, except where he makes a special study of it as an abnormality for dramatic effect. And in Hamlet and Timon we are shown a genuine disturbance of the spirit, the obverse of generous idealism, not to be compared for a moment with the mere melancholy temperament, or with the fantastic habit of melancholy. Bishop Hall may serve to toll the knell of the fashion in 1608, in his *Character of a Malcontent*, among his 'Vices':

Every eare is long agoe wearie of him, and he is almost wearie of himselfe. Give him but a little respit, and he will die alone; of no other death, than others' welfare.

Even the narrow circle of London literary society was weary of its Melancholy Man, who had never been seen walking abroad on the wider, truer English landscape.

Secondly, the whole notion that the early years of the reign of James were years of cynicism and of disillusionment is a feat of the delusive imagination, working backwards from a knowledge of the break-down of the Stuart monarchy under Charles, and encouraged by rhetorical distortions of the real personality of King James. All England is made to shamble with the shambling James, who is also accused of slobbering. It is true that King James was not a public-school boy. But then neither was Queen Elizabeth. The most recent study of King James, by a competent historian, opens with the words: 'Justice has never been done to James I, whether as a statesman or as a thinker.' The fact is that the mill-stone of nineteenth-century Whig history hangs heavy round our necks, condemning James unheard, because he was not a Whig. King James, as welcome a king as England has ever known, actually saved England from people like Essex, from civil war, and brought peace and increased prosperity. His accession dispelled the dangerous shadow that hung over the death-bed of Elizabeth, assuring the succession to the throne firmly, not only for his own life-time but also in two hopeful young princes, his sons. He solved the century-old problem of security from the North, and in his person created the United Kingdom. He made peace with Spain, and the whole country was freed of an incubus. Under James the establishment of England's colonial empire proceeded apace. Under James the Church of England found its true *via media*, and could give house-room and scope to so ardent and fiery a soul as John Donne. Under James the greatness of the English genius for literature in prose, verse, and drama became more manifest than ever before in the history of the nation. And under James the true foundations of modern English thought were laid.

Robert Burton, that detached and curious observer, who

wrote so fully upon the question of melancholy, has much
to say concerning the abuses and follies of the world which
he knew, but what he has to say on this count concerns the
world as a whole and humanity as a whole, nor is it limited
to contemporary times. And England in his eyes seems to
be in a far happier condition than the rest of his world in
his own day:

> We have besides many particular blessings, which our neigh-
> bours want, the Gospel truly preached, Church discipline estab-
> lished, long peace and quietness, free from exactions, foreign fears,
> invasions, domestical seditions, well manured, fortified by art and
> nature, and now most happy, in that fortunate union of *England*
> and *Scotland*, which our forefathers have laboured to effect, and
> desired to see. But in which we excel all others, a wise, learned,
> religious King, another *Numa*, a second *Augustus*, a true *Josiah*, most
> worthy senators, a learned clergy, an obedient commonalty, &c.

There are troubles in England, but they are like thistles in
a garden of 'many roses', disturbances of the general 'peace
of this body politick' and of its 'honour and glory'.

Here is, then, the view of a Jacobean Englishman of some
note, the fruit of his contemplations during the reign of
James, published towards its end, in 1621. What Burton
saw in retrospect of the reign, Francis Bacon saw in prospect
at the beginning of the reign.

To Bacon the reign of James seemed to have marked
'a full period of all instability and peregrinations', when
such great projects as he had formulated to himself under
Elizabeth, taking all knowledge to be his province, could
be fulfilled. It was an age when full profit could be taken
of all achievements of the past, both in the ancient and
modern worlds—an age of greater leisure, an age of peace
and freedom from controversy, an age when truth and
knowledge might come to their own,

> a rich storehouse for the glory of the Creator and the relief of man's
> estate,

in a conjunction of 'the two highest planets, Saturn, the
planet of rest and contemplation, and Jupiter, the planet

of civil society and action'. It was an age that was not un-worthy of such noble monuments as *The Advancement of Learning*, the Authorized Version of the Bible, and the tragedies of Shakespeare.

Let me turn to arguments that are more difficult to meet as being less subject to the decision of facts.

It is, for example, impossible to disprove that this or that play of Shakespeare is imbued with a spirit of disgust. It is a matter of individual feeling, of taste. But critical observations may well be offered when we consider the plays chosen as evidence of a mood of cynicism or of pessi-mism in Shakespeare, and as indications of the beginning, development, and terminus of such a mood.

I would insist, to begin with, that there is nothing in any of the plays that is not amenable to the conception of a great and disinterested poet and thinker in the process of dramatic creation, and little that is inexplicable save on the assump-tion of the reflection of direct personal experience and feel-ing, as distinct from the vast excitement and intensity of creative art. Shakespeare is throughout scrupulous to hold the balance even with 'right and wrong Between whose endless jars justice resides'. Who shall dare to say that the voice of Shakespeare is heard in the words of Gloucester:

> As Flies to wanton Boyes, are we to th'Gods,
> They kill us for their sport,

and is not heard in the words of Troilus, 'Think, we had mothers'? To what purpose is it to quote Iago's most loath-some suggestions to Othello, and to forget the heavenly attempt at deceit in which the dying Desdemona seeks to exonerate the husband who slew her, heart and body?

> *Emilia;* Oh who hath done this deed?
> *Desdemona;* No body: I my selfe, farewell:
> Commend me to my kinde Lord: oh farewell.

If this is to be disillusioned about woman-kind, may there be many to share Shakespeare's disillusionment!

The comedy of *Measure for Measure* has served as a text

for most of those who sorrow for and with Shakespeare. This play seems to be exceptionally distressing to a number of critics, and by a process of queer logic they attribute to Shakespeare their own distress and so conclude that it expresses a spirit of cynical revolt. Isabella in particular displeases them. Contemptuous words are written concerning 'the sainted Isabella, wrapt in her selfish chastity', or 'the rancid chastity of Isabella'. It is hard to be a woman and to please your true Puritan, for he disapproves no less of your unchaste woman, your Cleopatra, 'a libertine and a harlot', or your Cressida. Shakespeare should not have mentioned chastity at all, even though it were a matter truly of life and death not only to the Lucrece whom he celebrated in verse, but to any honest Elizabethan woman. It should not be forgotten that Shakespeare deliberately changed the old story, in which he found Isabella's chastity involved in ruin, and vainly sacrificed to a triumphant deceiver. And Shakespeare knew what he was doing when he set this steady star shining amid so much corruption.

Let there be no mistake about this; Shakespeare sets up Isabella as a heroine, who represents something in womanhood which Shakespeare, no less than Lucio in this play, reveres with all his heart. Nothing but a pseudo-romantic sentimentalism, utterly alien to the spirit of Shakespeare and of Elizabethan England, could fail to understand the rightness of Isabella and the reality of her dilemma. What we are pleased to call enlightenment to-day seeks to evade the embarrassing notion of sin, and is naturally anxious to enrol Shakespeare among its adepts. But sin, and deadly sin at that, is fundamental in Christian thought. If this is superstition, then both Hamlet and Isabella were superstitious. To Claudio's plea,

> Sure it is no sin;
> Or of the deadly seven it is the least,

she returns the only possible answer:

> Which is the least?

And Isabella was a novice of St. Clare. She could plead for mercy for Claudio, both from temporal and eternal justice, but could not pray for herself in like case. We must not pick and choose with Shakespeare's characters or with Christianity. We must not, for example, applaud Isabella's heavenly plea to Angelo on behalf of Claudio, because we approve of the Christian promise of mercy, and in the same breath condemn her faithfulness to what is no less integral a part of Christianity, though less fashionable to-day. In a word, it is Isabella's soul that is at stake. Her life she makes nothing of, and would be ready to sacrifice it for her brother 'as frankly as a pin'. To describe her, as does Professor Abercrombie, as a type of 'true puritanism', is to confuse puritanism with virtue, a confusion which Sir Toby indignantly reprehended. Change 'puritanism' to 'purity', and we are nearer the truth. The very rake Lucio in this play, who so deeply offends prudish refinement, is the most loyal of friends, and also venerates true virtue. Far from being rotten, the play is sound to the core, and profoundly Christian in spirit. Isabella is one of Shakespeare's greatest creations, hardly to be excelled among his characters of women even by Cleopatra. Incidentally, *Measure for Measure* with its superb dramatic poetry, diversified by comic force, and its absorbing theme, is one of Shakespeare's finest acting plays.

I have not space to answer for *All's Well that Ends Well*, for *Timon of Athens*, or for *Troilus and Cressida*, though I am ready with ample replies. I must be content with a few observations on especial points that have been exploited by various writers. In *All's Well*, for example, Parolles' dialogue upon virginity with Helena is much criticized. Yet the theme and the arguments furnished matter for an Address from Parliament to a greater lady than Helena, and are accepted without question in the form of sonnets by Shakespeare himself. The Elizabethans took the subject seriously. They were therefore able to handle it with the freedom of true wit, as here. And they were therefore free from such an obsession with sex as that which is alleged against Shakespeare. On this question the evidence of sanity and balance in these very plays is surely conclusive. It is, of course, possible to twist the words of Troilus, 'Think, we had mothers', into the opposite sense, despite the preceding words, 'let it not be believed for womanhood', and indeed the whole of the speech, with the reply of Ulysses. Why, even Wycherly knew better, when he made Sir Jasper Fidget reply to Horner,

For shame, Master Horner! Your mother was a Woman.

And Shakespeare's Timon, adduced as an example of the poet's disgust for woman, makes it his highest praise of the honest man, Flavius,

Surely this man was born of woman.

Timon, moreover, modifies his general condemnation of mankind in favour of women when he compares them, to their advantage, with the superior baseness of men, saying of flatterers 'women nearest, but men, men are the things themselves'. As for Timon's misanthropy, Shakespeare's preservation of his own balance may well be exemplified in the cold douche administered by Apemantus:

This is in thee a nature but infected,
A poor unmanly melancholy sprung
From change of fortune.

In *Troilus and Cressida* complex questions are involved. This, however, is certain, that the most tentative dipping into the vast field of medieval story of the matter of Troy, including the story of Troilus and Cressida, may well cast doubt upon the originality, the deliberateness, and the significance of Shakespeare's departure from pure heroics in his version of the theme. The last decade of the sixteenth century saw a marked revival of interest in the story of the Trojan War, as appears in stage history. And the Elizabethans had not lost the taste of their forbears for realism, for caricature, for mirth, as well as for romance, all characteristic of medieval versions and part of the traditional material held as it were in solution. The Greeks, moreover, had long been the butt of that Trojan bias which was proper to the citizens of Troynovant or New Troy.

Let us consider, again, the conflicting views concerning Cressida which appear elsewhere in Shakespeare. In *The Merchant of Venice*, as in *As You Like It*, we find Troilus and Cressida adduced as examples of great lovers in the world's history. In *Twelfth Night* and in *Henry the Fifth* we read of the broking of Pandarus and the leprosy that fell upon the faithless Cressida. Shakespeare had to set forth these two conflicting aspects of the story. He had to face the problem that so deeply concerned Chaucer and other medieval writers. In addition he had to develop all this, in the narrow limits of his dramatic form, as part of the wider field of the Trojan War. And there is more in it. Never did dramatist have thornier material to handle, in the attempt to set forth a play suitable for his stage and in reasonable agreement with common tradition and common knowledge of his theme.

With *Troilus and Cressida* above all, as also in other plays, it is in the main a question of the artistic problems which Shakespeare set himself, not of the problems which life set Shakespeare. There I must leave it, reluctantly. For here I have touched upon what ought to be a cardinal principle in all Shakespearian criticism, but is too often forgotten.

But let me carry the war into the opposing camp. It is a canon of the sorrowers' faith that Shakespeare's last plays are evidence of convalescence and cure, of a regained serenity and optimism. Yet if we are to seek texts expressive of the revolting side of humanity, I will engage to find them in plenty, and, indeed, Professor Dover Wilson has engaged himself to find them in *The Winter's Tale*, in *Cymbeline*, and even in *The Tempest*, to find the most unsparing pictures of ugly facts and ugly thoughts, and passages of bitterness of spirit to rival anything in *Troilus* or in *Timon*. There are nightmare moments, and more than moments, in these plays which have been described as 'happy dreams'. To take the matter deeper, however, what conclusion should be drawn from the spectacle of a poet who turns from the strict logic of events and character to the evasion of consequences in forced happy endings, as in *The Winter's Tale* or *Cymbeline*, in which the problems of *Othello*, leading in that play to appalling ends, are rehandled with poignancy and realism in their exposition? In the denouement of these plays, they fade away from realism into romance, and tragedy is turned into fairy tale. If we must look for weariness and lack of mastery of circumstance, we might well seek them rather in the 'Romances' than in *Lear* or *Othello*. There may truly be pleasure in the saving of the ship that wins through the storm safely to port in these last comedies. But it carries no cargo one-half so precious as that which is miraculously rescued from the foundering wreck in the great tragedies. For in them the very flag of humanity is left flying. The grand Enemy of mankind can do much. But with respect to certain immortal matters he is powerless to harm.

> Better is by evil still made better,

Herein lies in fact the essentially Christian spirit of the tragedies. It is strange indeed to have it called in question whether the spirit of Christianity is compatible with Tragedy, when Shakespeare stands to demonstrate the tragic illumination of that spirit in supreme grandeur. I would not hold that Shakespeare consciously sought to infuse a Christian outlook upon life and death into his tragedies, as I would not urge that he had in mind the parables so well illustrated by *Measure for Measure*. But a Christian interpretation of the world he lived in was in the very air he breathed, implicit in his modes of thought. Thus it comes that a parallel to that significance in his tragedy which differentiates it from the Stoic note of Chapman may well be found in the Christian story itself. The shadow of the Tree lies across his tragic scene. In that dark day when the Son of God, who was also Son of Man, hung upon the Cross, evil was in full cry of triumph. His enemies among his own people had vanquished him. The Roman power had crucified him. And presently there was nothing but weeping, and a tomb. But in this very destruction of his life and labour the great purpose was fulfilled, and out of his necessary sacrifice came the atonement and man's hope of salvation. Out of apparent ruin came precious gain, which could not otherwise have been attained. So with Shakespeare's Tragedies. The sense of reconciliation which remains to comfort us may well be called a sense of atonement. Once more,

> Better is by evil still made better,

and it was true of the Best also.

The Romances, like the Comedies, sail across less fatal seas than the Tragedies, but not with more courage or resolution, indeed with a more restricted optimism.

Let me observe further that there is no sort of consensus of opinion concerning the plays most in question. The conspirators are not agreed. For Brandes, *Antony and Cleopatra* has pessimism writ large in it. Brandes clearly did not like Cleopatra. But Sir Edmund Chambers is more kindly disposed, and according to him this play is evidence of a temporary recovery. *Timon of Athens*, to Brandes, Swinburne, Sir Edmund Chambers, and Professor Dover Wilson, is startlingly and terribly symptomatic of the break-down of the poet. But Dowden sees it as evidence of Shakespeare's regained mastery of himself. 'The impression which the play leaves is that of Shakespeare's sanity.' The pother about *Measure for Measure* is comparatively recent. August Schlegel declared its true significance to be 'the triumph of Mercy over strict justice', as indeed it is. Isabella was quite clear on the subject, long before Schlegel. As for 'the light or comick part', which seems so bitter to some, I am of the opinion of Dr. Johnson, that it is 'very natural and pleasing'. In fact, the play, to my mind, is worthy of its place in the rising curve of his dramatic power. To adapt another phrase of Dr. Johnson's, I urge that 'there

is perhaps not one of Shakespeare's plays more darkened
than this by the peculiarities of . . . its Editors'.

There is, again, the problem of chronology. Are we after
all satisfied that the chronology of the plays is sufficiently
established to allow of such exact deductions as have been
attempted? I need not elaborate this caution. It might
well be put much more strongly. Indeed, I fear that our
romantics may be accused of a circular process of argument. Such and such a play, we are told, is so sad that it
must belong to a certain year or thereabouts. And presently
we are to mark how sad Shakespeare was in that year, as may
be seen by the play thus dated. It is perhaps not too much
to say as Dr. Johnson said about certain Highlanders whose
assertions carried at first the compelling conviction of en-
chantment, that on further inquiry

it is discovered that what was told so confidently was told at
hazard, and that such fearlessness of assertion was either the sport
of negligence, or the refuge of ignorance.

The chronology of Shakespeare's personal development
offers even greater difficulties. The process of change is
curiously rapid, if we are to accept the general account.
We have no external knowledge whatever of Shakespeare's
real youth, except his early marriage. He was twenty-eight
when we first hear of him in London, and already well
known there. His 'gay' comedies, so redolent of youth, were
still occupying him when he was approaching the age of
forty, were, in fact, the work of middle age. Yet by the
time he has written *The Tempest*, when he was at most
forty-seven, he appears suddenly as an old man. He has
now retired to Stratford, a statement unsupported by evidence, as is the notion that he ever retired from Stratford,
that he ever ceased to continue in touch with Stratford and
his family there. And he is now, only seven years after his
long-enduring youth, represented as serene, as immovably
complacent, as befits his advanced years. There is something wrong with either this youth, or this old age, or with
both.

We may well challenge, moreover, the notion that a man, in the late twenties even, is likely to write gay literature because he is in the late twenties and is therefore gay. If you wish to find desperate stuff in poetry you will do well to seek it in the writings of young poets: Goethe was twenty-five when he started *The Sorrows of Young Werther*. And when Coleridge was about the same age as Shakespeare at the beginning of his 'gay' period, at the age of thirty, he was busy writing *Dejection, an Ode*. If, moreover, we wish to find a mood of cynicism concerning women in Shakespeare, we should have no difficulty in making out a case for *Richard the Third*, written when he was not more than thirty years of age. And much might be said against the further notion that with maturing years comes a darker view of life. But the real heresy lies more deeply embedded, rooted in a false aesthetic theory of Shakespeare's tragic inspiration.

I am very far from conceding the proposition that tragic writing in a great creative writer is evidence of a tragic mood, or of private unhappiness of any kind. 'When a man is unhappy', remarked Coleridge to Southey, 'he writes damned bad poetry.' Thomas Hardy, who was a cheerful soul in his private life, was once asked why he was not equally cheerful in his novels. His reply was that you cannot make such good books about cheerful people. And here we have, in fact, the true key to the problem of what is called Shakespeare's Tragic Period, the true answer to the question why Shakespeare turned to writing the great tragedies. If the explanation we have so often been offered is the true explanation, and Shakespeare himself is speaking by the mouth of Gloucester, then I would be bound to apply to the poet the opinion of Farmer Dobson, in Tennyson's play, concerning Gloucester:

Edgar. 'What are we', says the blind old man in Lear?
      'As flies to the Gods; they kill us for their sport '
Farmer Dobson (aside). Then the owd man i' Lear should be
   shaämed of hissen.

As for the notion that Shakespeare's tragedy is the inevitable reflection of a period of national degradation, its absurdity may be seen in reference to the natural parallel of the world's greatest dramatic poetry other than the English, in the history of Greek tragedy. There, too, we have had the myth-making craze at work, as in the inventions of scholiasts which embroidered on the life of the tragedian Phrynichus. We could readily work the tragedies of Sophocles also into a highly coloured picture of the crises of his spiritual life. With him, we might plausibly proceed, the time of suffering and storm came early, instigating the despairing mood of *Ajax*, and culminating in *Oedipus Tyrannus*. In *Oedipus Coloneus* we see the return to a calmer spirit. And in one of the latest of his plays, *Philoctetes*, we have the evidence of his final mood of magnificent fortitude and constancy, with the character of Neoptolemus to illustrate the kindly tenderness of the poet in his old age. Did we but possess the whole of his output of tragedy, instead of mere samples, we might have a complete picture, it might be argued. But we know in fact that the life of Sophocles, as far as our information goes, opposes any such fanciful theories.

So with any attempt to relate the tragedies of Sophocles to the history of his country. It is impossible to refer his greatness and his poignancy to the degradation of Athens. In the days of the splendour of Pericles, as in the days of the Peloponnesian War, Sophocles was writing noble tragedy. He died before the fatal battle of Aegospotami. But it was when the coming storm was looming closer that he wrote *Philoctetes*, in which there is no shadow of gloom or cynicism. Shakespeare himself, indeed, has a word applicable to that notion of drama which would make the dramatist

> some fierce thing replete with too much rage,
> Whose strength's abundance weakens his own heart.
>
> (Sonnet XXIII.)

It is Aeschylus, Sophocles, and Euripides, with Seneca,

observe, the great tragedians of classical literature, that Ben Jonson first calls forth as parallels to Shakespeare. And to Holland and Basse, for example, among his other eulogists in the First Folio, Shakespeare is above all the 'rare Tragoedian'. In Elizabethan eyes the test of greatness in drama was, in fact, tragedy, as we may well see in their critical writings. Sidney has to defend comedy in its right use; but 'high and excellent Tragedy' is safe from attack. Tragedy could not fail to be 'unpleasant', for it is its very function to 'open the greatest wounds', to portray the more deadly aspects of human vice and error, as compared with the 'base matter' of comedy in Puttenham's view. There is no need to seek further for explanation of the poignancy of Shakespeare's tragedy, except to allow for the gifts of the greatest of dramatists. And there is no doubt that Tragedy had a higher standing as literature. 'Tragedies well handled be a most worthie kind of Poesie', wrote Harington. 'The stately Tragedie scorneth the trifling Comedie', wrote Gabriel Harvey. And Marston, a dramatist, makes the point abundantly clear between 1604 and 1606. When he prints a comedy he is apologetic; such things are for the stage and for the moment; they depend for their life on 'the soul of lively acting', and are 'trifles in reading'; 'slight easy labours in this hasty play'. But he thinks very differently of tragedy: 'I will present a tragedy to you, which shall boldly abide the most curious perusal'; and when he prints *Sophonisba* it is a 'poem', written by him not 'as an historian' but 'as a poet'. In 1612 Webster, again, makes a marked distinction in commenting upon the audiences at the Red Bull, and writes of 'that which is the onely grace and setting out of a Tragedy, a full and understanding Auditory'. So with Shakespeare. If he is to prove himself in drama to be a true poet, it must be in tragedy. If he is to share in drama the greatness of his friend Ben Jonson, he must rival him in tragedy. If the King's Men are to maintain their supremacy, both as a company of actors and as an integral part of the London world of culture, they must have tragedy. The

Shakespeare who in earlier years found artistic satisfaction
in the craftsmanship of *Venus and Adonis* was now a riper,
fuller man, conscious of his powers, determined to come to
grips with greater matters and to fulfil his destiny, with a
passion to excel in his chosen field of creation. And the
ambition of his fellow-actors of the great King's Company,
encouraged by the literary taste of the time in closer touch
than ever with the theatre, urged him on in this inevitable
scaling of the greater heights of drama. So it was, and not
otherwise, that, in the words of Malone,

the genius of our great poet gradually expanded itself, till, like
his own Ariel, *it flamed amazement* in every quarter.

Shakespeare had written tragedies as well as poems in the
earlier stages of his career, but we do not have *Titus Andronicus, Romeo and Juliet*, or *Richard the Third*, that very cynical
play, brought forward as evidence of any preliminary sorrows. It saves trouble to cast out *Titus Andronicus* from the
canon, in spite of the irrefutable evidence. But *Titus Andronicus* is a vastly important play. It shows us Shakespeare
the poet, following his literary ambitions on the stage as
well as in heroic poems at this early date. Senecan tragedy
was still an accepted model of dramatic literature, and
Shakespeare was trying his prentice hand in the higher
flights. He has not yet found himself, and his art is still
capable of being dominated by influences external to himself, in an age that was deeply subject to literary authority.
In the later period he set his 'proud full sail' in a ship of his
own building. But we should beware of dismissing *Titus
Andronicus* carelessly as a sop thrown to the Cerberus of
sensationalism by a journeyman hackwriter. It is really the
proof that the player Shakespeare was already setting up
claims to be considered as a poet-dramatist, essaying the
manner that Sidney prescribed. This is no private dis-
covery. Shakespeare was widely enough known before 1600
as a poet of promise and of achievement, in his printed
poems, in his stage-plays, and in his sonnets circulated

among his friends in manuscript. His career, seen as a whole, and in its true light, is as much the career of a poet and an artist as that of a purveyor for the stage. We have, in the past, accepted much too readily the theory of the divorce of the stage from literature, even in the Elizabethan period of the drama, when the writer of a play was after all, in common parlance, a 'poet'.

What alternative is there to this view of Shakespeare's artistic career? None but the oldest of all fallacies about Shakespeare, over three hundred years old, restated in more sophisticated language in the light of the Romantic Age of literature, Milton's uncritical, if loving, fancy of Shakespeare's 'native woodnotes wild', swelling into the prolonged chorus that praised his Nature and neglected his Art, and at last booming through the loud-speaker of *Sturm und Drang*; the refusal to recognize in Shakespeare the master-mind, the supreme craftsman and artist, not controlled by, but controlling, his genius, as great by virtue of his command of thought as by dint of his creative art, by the immense balance and sanity of his outlook upon man and the world of men.

Why should we deny to Shakespeare the moral and intellectual strength that we acknowledge in his great contemporary Cervantes, whose real and desperate vicissitudes in life we know, and whose constancy and good temper never failed? For my part I cannot away with any image of Shakespeare which represents him as an impatient Job, smitten with sore boils, sitting down among the ashes, and taking the drama unto himself as a potsherd to scrape himself withal. *Ubi dolor, ibi digitus*, will not serve our turn here.

Shakespeare was not stung into tragedy by any Dark Lady. He was not depressed into tragedy by the fall of Essex, who threatened revolution and chaos in England, to Shakespeare's horror and alarm; the cruelty of anarchy was a thought that haunted the poet like a nightmare. He did not degenerate into tragedy in a semi-delirium of cynicism and melancholy, ending in a religious crisis. Shakespeare *rose* to tragedy in the very height and peak of his powers, nowhere else so splendidly displayed, and maintained throughout his robust and transcendent faith in God and his creature Man. This is the first article of my creed concerning Shakespeare as man and as artist. He experienced and faced the twin problems of pain and of evil in no spirit of petulance, but with an insight into immanent good of which the tragedies are the clearest proof. Such a conception of Shakespeare's spiritual life is at least not less consistent with his written work and with the known facts of his life, than that which manufactures the tragi-comedy of his mythical sorrows out of straws blowing in the wind of his sovereign genius.